The House in the Forest

First published 2020 by The Hedgehog Poetry Press

Published in the UK by
The Hedgehog Poetry Press
5, Coppack House
Churchill Avenue
Clevedon
BS21 6QW

www.hedgehogpress.co.uk

ISBN: 978-1-913499-11-2

A CIP Catalogue record for this book is available from the British
Library.

Contents:

MICK YATES

Séance

so here i am fourteen years old in an upstairs room in the derelict house

where a strange man once lived who ran a hospital for damaged dolls

the place where he mended the broken dolls of children and healed them all

a haunted place many locals say in hushed tones

yet here we sit quite innocently and prepare for our Ouija board session

the ragged curtains are drawn as we consult the board

through the dust and remnants of a life long since departed from this world

and where we hope to receive a message from beyond the grave

suddenly we see and smell cigar smoke blue and acrid in the air

is it our young imaginations or is it for real?

the pointer on the Ouija board runs wild footsteps echo on the stairs

the summer sun ceases to shine through the broken windows

we hear the deep voice of a man echoing around the room speaking in tongues

is this our collective hysteria or something else?

the cigar smoke gets thicker and more pungent hanging in the air like shrouds

all at once we do not wish to meet the dead anymore

we run down the rickety steps as quickly as we can out through the front door

where we breathe in the fresh air and savour the summer sun once more

far away from the other realm we glimpsed darkly and briefly in the house

back to the innocence of youth chastened and glad to be alive in the real world once again

OZ HARDWICK

Desirable Property

As she moves from room to room, the woman is aware of the changing scents; from fire to damp, to the bay hedge that leans from the black and white photograph that hangs beside the window. It used to lie as flat as an early 60s Sunday in provincial England, but since her parents died it has become unruly, bristling into her aimless wanderings. Where the branches thin to bitten nails, she glimpses the great house, white as hospital sunlight, rebuilt since the war, with all its children rushing through corridors. Stepping into the long window, she shrinks under the eyes of someone else's disapproving ancestors, all sneering beneath blasted figs with their sleek hounds and horses. The gallery smells of the sea and split pine, and of the bay hedge that leans from the mirror in which the woman now regards herself, aged seventeen or eighteen, in the window of a provincial house, black as a hospital lift shaft, that was flattened in the war. Away, up countless stairs, she hears the splash of children in a picture of an ornate fountain. She turns to follow, but the room moves around her.

NAOMI STERLING

The Gingerbread House (Post-Genocide)1

After the war, it seemed mad not to continue what we'd begun.

My husband does not enter the kitchen,
nor question the meat from which his meal is made.
And besides, you can develop a taste for human flesh.

We live in the borderlands.
People come here to disappear.
The fighting was bad round about, but we were not disturbed:
our thatched hut hardly distinguishable from the soil that surrounds.

Survivors wander in, sometimes.
But when all else are dead, who will miss them?
I know the value of certain herbs, seeds.
A healing brew can lead to lasting sleep.

I tell my man they moved on – many do –
and that night we eat meat:
a rich stew, scented and spiced,
fatty and fulfilling.

Why let good food go to waste?

I know one day my time will come:
a knock at the door, a push, a shove,
and then the flames.

But given what we have seen on earth,
what I have done,
what need I fear of hell?

---

1 During the 1994 Genocide in Rwanda, some accounts of cannibalism were reported, both of murderers roasting and eating the hearts of those they killed; and of those fleeing death and/or in hiding forced to eat parts of dead bodies in order to survive.
In subsequent years, occasional stories made the local news of couples or individuals, usually from isolated, rural parts of the country, continuing the practice. The second stanza paraphrases one couple's explanation/justification of the wife's actions (the husband claimed ignorance).

ANDREW STICKLAND

Shallow Graves

I struggle all through the wet heat of afternoon.
Beneath another year of weeds and ferns the earth
is dark and soft, and smells like childhood,

but the roots are tough and tangled, and that
same old shovel is rusty now, and blunt
from all the work of all those summers past.

As usual, the family have come to watch me work.
Ma stands at the top window, arms folded
across the front of her dress to hide the stain.

Behind her, his loving hand on her shoulder, is Pa.
The back of his skull is lost in the gloom,
but always such disappointment in his eyes.

Off to the side is dear little, sweet little, Rose,
face so pale, eyes so dark and empty,
her long hair still running wet from the lake.

I straighten up for the sake of my back,
turn to the house and wave, but unmoving,
they dissolve into sunlight and shade.

The others will come later, picking their silent way
through the elongated fingers of sunset,
each with their untold story of sadness and horror,

and when I'm done for the day, and washed
and changed, and sat by the stove,
then they will gather at the windows,

dead hands and dead faces pressed to the glass,
sightless, searching for that thing they've lost,
finding nothing.

Today's secrets were laid to rest in shallow graves,
plastic-wrapped against the coyotes and wolves,
but the heat and the moisture will see to their needs

soon enough, and soon enough these new memories
will pick themselves up from the dirt, find their way
to the front porch, to the old wooden seat

where they will wait for me each morning, the fear
and confusion running in scarlet rivulets down pale flesh
until it seeps away between their entwined fingers,

until the late-morning sun chases them away,
back into the shadows, back into the dark soil
that smells of childhood, and keeps so many secrets.

The house is getting crowded.
I still come up each summer.
Sometimes I bring guests.

ANDY EYCOTT

Deep in the Forest

Mice run skittish into corners,
dust grey as the bare boards
they cross in a breath.

There is a presence here,
the air charged with secrecy,
heavy with dandruff of a beaten rug,

yet no sign of beater or rug.
No sign of life yet a creek,
aching bones in boarded walls,

catches a cautious ear. The clock
in my chest ticking irregular time,
I shouldn't have come.

Elusive, the journey's path through
the waving fronds of ferns, wands
weaving a memory spell.

A cold pot belly, rain-streaked fog
clouding lenses, eyes to the forest.
A sense of something absent.

The front door firm, striped with splintered
wounds, I observe signs of pure animal fury,
notice an ancient iron lock without a key.

BRIAN MCMANUS

Fallen Angels

Sheltered by trees at the side of a loch
stands a house always shrouded in darkness.
Conjured up devils, the Princes of Hell
stalk a world steeped in putrid catharsis.

Belial, Satan and all of their kin,
brooding angels of rancid destruction.
Cast out of heaven they aim to return
with a programme of rape and abduction.

Decades ago they had gutted a church
bringing fire and flame and disaster.
Worshippers screamed as they burned alive
while the demons watched screaming with laughter.

In the crypt of the sacred old graveyard
the choirmaster smirks while spending his seed.
As the residents rot in their coffins,
the beleaguered world continues to bleed.

Inside the house in the dead of the night
doors will crash and the furniture scatter.
The locals bereft, they cower in fear,
with their children gone, life doesn't matter.

No stairway to heaven descends in this game,
devil's work goes on, the song remains the same.

PHIL SANTUS

Goldilocks

If you are Goldilocks,
then what are you thinking
when you enter into
the strange and quiet house?

When you try the porridge
and you find that its warm,
does it not make you think
who has just departed?

Does the significance
not dawn on you, sweet child,
of three chairs and three beds?
Could you be outnumbered?

Is your hunger so great
that you resort to theft
and also to trespass
and criminal damage?

You awake in the bed,
see unnatural bears,
and manage to escape,
screaming and traumatised.

Do take comfort, my child,
it could have been far worse.
They could have been humans,
alerting the police.

SUSAN DARLINGTON

The Last In A Long Line

I'm the last in a long line of ghosts.
Of women whose bloom grew diseased
under the heat of the glasshouse;
who lost their minds and scuttled
barefoot over forks after being told
that *no* meant *yes* all their lives;
whose blood ran down their legs
and was washed from view down drains
after a crochet hook and too hot bath.

I'm the last in a long line of ghosts
who've fought to dismantle this house
and exorcise those who've lived here;
whose matrilineal scars weakened its foundations
and shook its dusty, cracked windows
until its inhabitants woke from dreamless sleep.
Now I want you to have the courage
to enter and help me build it anew
brick
        by
      hopeful
        brick.

MARGARET ROYALL

An Uncanny Forest Discovery

Thick foliage, treacle dark and dense
overhanging a dirt track like a punk chick's
lipstick slash, threading through forest.

Carve through dense briars with your dervish
blade, tread down the devil's thorny spines,
crawl belly-flat through a slough of despair.

Once through, a clearing beckons with lush
carpet of jade green velvet. But beware!
A false lure, an illusion! Don't trust your eyes!

From here you might catch the first drone
of distant machinery, see the kettle-black plume
of toxic fumes rising from an old smoke stack;

a throwback to the old satanic mills,
warning enough for the intrepid that
further investigation will not end well!

Only one mortal ever lived to sketch this den
of iniquity, where barghests, dybbuks and chimeras
are magicked back to full demonic power!

Briefly he returned! But his shrivelled corpse
was pulled next day from a quarry, feet tied to
huge boulders, face green with foaming slime,

heart missing, ripped from a pulverised rib cage.
They say he peered in through gaps in the barred
windows, witnessed such scenes of depravity

as struck him blind deaf and dumb; a quivering,
howling heap, eyes wild like a madman escaped
from an asylum, his forked tongue spitting fire.

No birds fly near nor dare to perch and sing,
no fox slinks by, no rabbit or creature ventures
within a mile. The air exhales a veiled threat...

You'll see local children dance in a ring, hold hands,
sing with false bravado a rhyme their ancestors sang:

'If you wander the woods today
You'll probably not come back, they say,
For evil creatures await you there
To gobble up skin and bones and hair.
Will you come with us bye and bye?
We quickly answer: No, not I'

MERRIL D. SMITH

For Luck

At the rowan tree,
I put a berry in my pocket

for luck, I said,
and laughed--

two friends, an impulsive decision,
a mythical vision,

before the small glimmering spheres appeared
beckoning in a pulsing dance to follow,

and we did--slipping
through stands of centuries-old oaks,

where with branches raised in supplication, or command
to stop here, in this strangely silent space

before the house with ancient beams and weathered stone,
bone-white in tree-slivered, silvered light,

moss, like a fringe around its window-eyes, watching
our figures reflected in wavy glass, connected,

somehow to others--from inside--
gazing out.

Quick, look away, I say,
don't let it know you've seen them.

Too late.
Was there a cry?

A baby, he said.
A baby, I'm sure.

Or was it a woman—
someone in distress.

And so, he left on a quest, to search, to save--
always the hero--while I stayed--

I tried to stop him—or at least to wait--
I did—I did—I did--

then felt a small, cold hand take mine,
saw two eyes, shine black—or—green--

a color I've never before seen,
from a small, pale face floating in the darkness.

Come with me—and I started to--
but something took me from my trance,

a burning in my pocket, perhaps,
I screamed, maybe, it's all a blur,

and I whirled, stumbling over massive, rambling roots, I ran,
leaving a stink of festering fright--

though I heard the forest's whispered taunt
leave him to his fate tonight.

Now, in my dreams, I see the house
and there, my lost, last friend,

who with glowing eyes and rictus grin, murmurs,
I can't wait to see you again.

PATRICIA M. OSBORNE

Campfire Horror

Rick nudges Peter.

The cub scouts creep away
from the glowing campfire
into the still silence,
tiptoeing in darkness
through an oak grove
to the derelict mansion
deep in the forest.

Rick pushes   open
the squeaky door,
they step inside.
Peter flicks his torch
as the boys climb
                         the creaky stairs,
                    shining a beam
   on each splintered tread.

Wind whistles down the chimney,
Peter shoots   light
into dust-filled darkness,
Rick shivers, coughs – wheezes.

A rat-like shape scratches floor boards
it scurries off into shadows.

Peter bangs a battered chest,
Rick opens the domed lid,
hinges creak, dried droppings rattle.

Peter screams as a huge hairy spider
       crawls   over his ankle.

Rick's spine stiffens. He turns–
A demon face with massive teeth
       launches towards him.

Peter races
              downstairs
                    Rick chases close behind.
       Lightning flickers, thunder crashes,
creaking   beams   crack.

Rick trips short of the door,
Peter stretches out his hand
as a blast of rubble
                  cascades.

AMINA ALYAL

Laying a ghost

Do come in. Meet my friend
that I mentioned. Well, *friend*
is a bit presumptuous. We've only
just met, haven't we? Well, since you –
you've been
lingering
here now ever since I came here
on retreat, to get away,
but I only saw you, didn't I,
last time it was
not very light.

Yes, so as I was saying
about my friend here -
this is someone who has -

it was something I wanted
not to remember
and my friend here
has brought it back
and might take some
persuading
to
be encouraged
to go home.
It might take some
actions
and some
ingredients
if you know what I mean.

Well, my friend is changed
by a process of
stasis -
shall we say stasis?
So the point is, I was
wondering if - can you
try the
encouragement process?
My friend here
won't mind me saying -
it gets quite dull here
and it's not the sort of place fit to entertain a
changed
person. A person beyond stasis.

DARREN J BEANEY

Sidney instead

A scuttle through dense woods on the limits
of Stray City, heading home. Copper basket
in hand, full of plastic pickles
and someone's flimsy laundry,   counterfeit bonanza.

Titan trees act like atrocious flypaper
tacky with trench-foot quicksand, hiding
barrels of stray dogs dumped
by an offside bartender.

Ears hustle, slaves to boombox
glow. Acidic harmony conjured by bandit wizards,
high on nitro jelly and Grimm tales.

Senses dumbfounded by hipster invasion.
Big bad bearded wolves pause
me in my tracks.   My way barred.

All is inflamed.   Velvet woodland ground.   Blistered sky.
  My bloodshot dominant eye.
Goldilocks
and her off-colour hood
cannot salvage me now.

KATHRYN ALDERMAN

The House of Dark Hearts

And it happens that you stumble
over that pock in the woods
you'd hoped never to see again.

That sudden murk of light,
the lowest note yowting,
a horde of totems crowing
over the house that hate built.

You brace for the scald
of its breath, its finger-point glare,
would run but your feet
are gripped in fists of fern.

Demon windows rattle and flex;
bulge-eyed arbiters
of the cut of your skin,
what breed of thing,
your lores and loves.

Found wanting and they'll fire
the gnaw-bone flume
to whistle up the hounds.

This is not your tribe,
these dark hearts cloning ghouls.
Yours is free as minds,
with charms to tumble walls.

You'll pocket a truth stone,
target this devil sight,
shatter its nightmare vision.

KATE YOUNG

Woven in your Fabric

Back from the wake you breathe
the darkness from your soul,
your skin a-quiver beneath quilt
as the house settles for the night.

Moonshine intrudes, slips inside
your first ragged sleep this year,
a lichen creeping through veins
and walls. I hold you close,

drag you from half-baked dreams
screaming into cockcrow,
arms a-flay as you swim to surface
seconds too late, eyes misting.

I am elastic, still stretching ways
to keep you elusively close.
Can you feel my fluidity?
The shapeless drift of time stalling?

I conceal myself well,
laced in splinters of memory.
You weave your grief as tapestry,
pull a thread, I fear you may unravel.

Sometimes, you catch my voice
in the chuckle of summer mowing
and trace my scent back
to the tumble-towel warmth

of spring   rising   softly.
I hover over lilies laid to rest
on the grave you visit briefly,
but never seem to leave.

I am woven in your fabric.
Look around, feel the shadow-slip?
Eyes slide over the bone-obvious,
sleep takes you, folds you over.

ROSIE BARRETT

Shh...Are You Sure You're All Alone?

Are you sure there's nothing there?
That creak outside your door?

It's nothing. Don't worry.
It's just the gone-befores
the baby who didn't thrive
her mother who   this time
did not survive.

That pitta pat late at night
not rain   nor dripping tap.

Don't fret. Don't worry
they were here first.
They won't hurt you
the granny who lived
a long   long life
the young man
back from the war.

Don't worry they're
in another time and space.

Yes   you can feel them.
Yes   you know they're there.
Ask them nicely to move on.
Say *Go in Peace.*
They might.

PHILIPPA HATTON-LEPINE

Photographing Ghosts

From a distance it is a skeleton
soulless windows
rooms dark as their stories.

Close up, I notice the silence
sudden and total, echoes frozen
as though heavy snow has fallen.
My imagination plays too loud
without distractions -
anechoic madness for those who stay too long.

Inside, the wrongness is biblical
forbidden words once spoken
have caused an unbecoming,
nothing natural can exist here.
I place the camera on a ledge
then leave. I don't call out.

Outside, I run, rubbing the tickling dread
from my back. The traffic on the road ahead
hums a welcoming hymn. I fear
my reflection in the rear view mirror.

Once home, everything is too bright,
internally lit, cut out, replaced with sharpness
clear as new glasses, cruel as high-definition.
I dream of decapitated animals, covering my lawn
in wet black trails, I wake crying at the loss.

At the old house, my camera starts filming.